# IN SEARCH OF THE UNEXPLAINED

# BIGFOOT

by Jenna Lee Gleisner

Kaleidoscope
Minneapolis, MN

# BIGFOOT
## BOOKS

### *The Quest for Discovery Never Ends*

· · · · · · · · · · · · · · · · · · · · · · · · · · · · · · · · · · · · · · · · · · · ·

*This edition first published in 2022 by Kaleidoscope Publishing, Inc.*

*No part of this publication may be reproduced in whole or in part without written permission of the publisher.*

*For information regarding permission, write to Kaleidoscope Publishing, Inc.*
*6012 Blue Circle Drive*
*Minnetonka, MN 55343*

*Library of Congress Control Number*
*2021934873*

*ISBN*
*978-1-64519-483-5 (library bound)*
*978-1-64519-521-4 (ebook)*

*Printed in the United States of America.*

**FIND ME IF YOU CAN!**

Bigfoot lurks within one of the images in this book. It's up to you to find him!

# TABLE OF
# CONTENTS

# GLOWING RED EYES

**D**eep in the Gifford Pinchot National Forest, night falls upon two hikers. This forest covers more than one million acres (4,050 square kilometers) of Washington state. The hikers have hiked in many forests. But they're new to the Pacific Northwest and these **remote** woods. Turned around, and with darkness setting in, they decide to set up camp for the night.

Just as they get their fire started, the sound of snapping trees fills the forest. Something large is crashing through the woods. And whatever it is is getting closer. The crashing suddenly stops. The forest goes quiet. The hikers look out into the darkness. They see two red eyes glowing back at them. Before they can turn on their flashlights, the eyes vanish. Whatever large creature just saw them is gone. Did they just look into the eyes of Bigfoot?

# ONE STEP AHEAD

Reports of a so-called Bigfoot or Sasquatch date back to the early 1800s. David Thompson was a British explorer. In 1811, he discovered giant footprints in Canada. Near Oregon, settlers claimed to have seen hairy, wild men as early as 1904. Twenty years later, miners on Mount St. Helens said they were attacked by what they called giant apes. Thousands of people claim to have seen, heard, and even smelled Bigfoot. But hardly any **evidence** has been gathered. Is Bigfoot just a **legend**? Or do these creatures really exist? And if they do, why can't we find them? Decide for yourself as we go in search of the unexplained!

**FUN FACT**

Bigfoot is also called Sasquatch. Sasquatch means "wild men" in Salish. The Salish are a group of American Indians of the Pacific Northwest.

The legend of Bigfoot has been around for centuries. But he, or his kind, is **elusive**. Humans haven't been able to find Bigfoot—or much evidence to prove he exists. One of the few traces he does leave behind is footprints. The first reported set was in 1958. Men on a construction crew in Northern California found footprints. They looked like human footprints, but they were huge. They measured 16 inches (41 centimeters) long. What kind of creature had human-like feet that large?

## BIGFOOT FOOT SIZE 16 INCHES
(41 cm)

## AVERAGE HUMAN FOOT SIZE 10 INCHES
(25 cm)

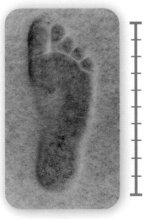

In 1967, arguably the most famous shot of Bigfoot was recorded on film. Roger Patterson and Bob Gimlin were riding on horseback through Bluff Creek, California, when Roger's camera captured a shot of something almost unbelievable. A tall, dark-haired creature walked across a creek. It walked on two feet, and its long arms hung at its sides.

Deer are thought to be Bigfoot's main source of food. Wherever deer are, Bigfoot is thought to follow.

# HUMAN-FREE FORESTS

Most reports of Bigfoot are from the northwestern United States and western Canada. Why? Forests cover much of this area. Forests, with their thick growth, serve as great camouflage. But most importantly, these areas are often remote. Few humans live in these forests. What better place for smart but shy creatures to live?

# Chapter 2

# BIG BIPED

The date is October 23, 2010. A deer hunter heads to his favorite hunting spot. It is just after 7:00 a.m. The woods are still dark. He quietly walks on a trail when he notices a large animal ahead. It walks with very long, big steps. It doesn't make any noise.

The hunter turns on his flashlight to get a better look. What he sees makes his hair stand on end. The creature stands over seven feet (2.1 meters) tall. It is covered in dark fur and has a muscular build. The hunter thinks it must weigh around 500 pounds (230 kilograms). Before he can get a photo, the creature slides down a hill and out of sight.

All accounts of Bigfoot, including the footprints, tell us he is a **biped**. Like humans, Bigfoot stands upright. He walks on two feet. He shares other features with humans as well.

*A Neanderthal*

## DISTANT RELATIVES

Studies show that modern humans lived at the same time as Neanderthals. We overlapped with other human species, too. This could have happened as recently as 30,000 years ago. And there are still many unknowns in the human family tree. What does this mean? Another species of humans could exist. And it could look a lot like Bigfoot. This would help explain Bigfoot's intelligence. Maybe that is how it's been able to hide for so long.

# BIGFOOT

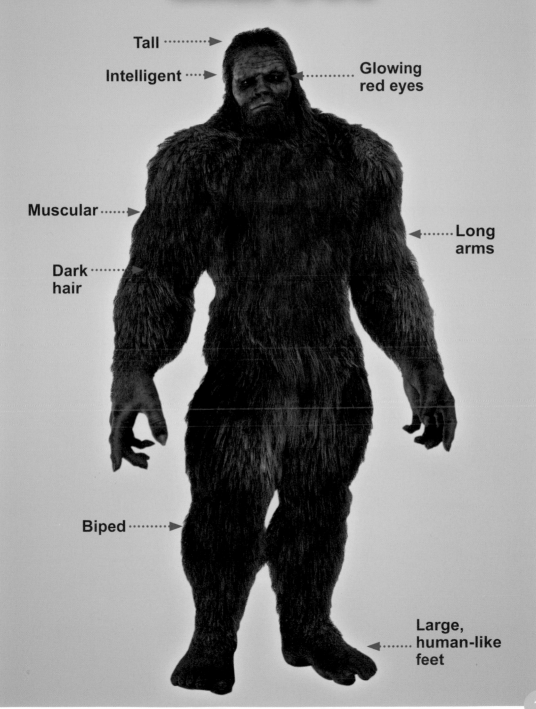

Tall

Intelligent

Glowing red eyes

Muscular

Long arms

Dark hair

Biped

Large, human-like feet

# Chapter 3

# SCREAMS AND KNOCKING

**A** group of scouts sits around their nightly fire. This is their favorite spot in the Oregon woods. They camp here every summer.

"I'm roasting another marshmallow. Pass me that stick." Just as the scout and his troop are about to enjoy s'mores, they hear a high-pitched scream. It cuts through the woods.

"What was that?" asks one boy, his eyes widening.

"Didn't sound like any animal we've heard before…" says the scoutmaster. "Everyone, in your tents. Now."

The boys stayed up all night, waiting to hear the scream again. But it never came.

**FUN FACT**
There have been 1,800 Bigfoot sightings in Oregon alone over the past 50 years.

Bigfoot hunters use similar calls. They also use long, loud howls. Bigfoot is thought to be a **territorial** species. If called to in the wild, it may call back. Why? People think it wants to let you know it's there. The call serves as a warning. It says, "stay away." It could also think it's calling back to another Bigfoot. Hunters call to see if it will call back. Then they can try to track it.

A cougar

# BIGFOOT OR ANIMAL?

Many say Bigfoot's screams are high-pitched. They are said to sound like a woman's screams. But could it be an animal? Bigfoot territory is home to many animals. These include cougars and red foxes. Both of these animals make loud, screeching sounds.

A red fox

Bigfoot is said to make sounds such as screams, howls, and even whistles. It will also produce sounds. One of these is wood knocking. They hit rocks or thick branches against trees. This loud sound echoes through the forest. Like the screams, it is thought to warn people to stay away. Or it's a method of **communicating** with other Bigfoots.

## SQUATCHY BEHAVIOR

With its size and build, Bigfoot would be very strong. People think Bigfoot likes to show this by lifting and throwing objects. Some claim large rocks have been hurled at them. Others claim Bigfoot has lifted their mobile homes and cars.

# Chapter 4

# FINDING BIGFOOT

Reports of Bigfoot don't come only from the woods or mountains. In fact, people say they have spotted him in the swamps of Florida. On a May morning in 2011, a guide and two men were fishing in a mangrove swamp. On the shore, they saw what they thought could be a hog or bear. But as they drifted closer, the creature stood up tall. The guide claimed it had a beard and a bare forehead. It was as wide as a refrigerator. It stared right at them for just seconds. Then it walked away into the mangroves.

**FUN FACT**

In Florida, Bigfoot is called the "Skunk Ape." Reports around the country say Bigfoot has a foul smell. It smells like a skunk or rotting animal.

*A skunk*

Bigfoot sightings take place around the country. Bigfoot Field Researchers Organization lists at least one report from every state, except Hawaii, over the past two decades. So why can't we find any **DNA**? Some believe it is because Bigfoot is an **apex predator**. Apex predators leave little evidence. Why? Since they aren't hunted, they likely die naturally. It is thought that Bigfoots die in their nests, which are hidden.

**It is believed that Bigfoots build shelters. Bigfoot hunters have come across large nests. They are usually built with ferns, moss, and grasses.**

MOST
SIGHTINGS

LEAST
SIGHTINGS

All we have are blurry photographs, one video, and accounts without evidence. But people who claim to have seen Bigfoot believe he exists. And many are terrified to retell their tale. So what did they see, hear, or smell? Was it just a wild animal? Their imaginations? Or does a human-like species exist out there? Are you a Bigfoot believer? Would you go in search of Bigfoot?

# BEYOND THE BOOK

After reading the book, it's time to think about what you learned. Try the following exercises to jump-start your ideas.

## THINK

**FIND OUT MORE.** There is so much more to dig up about Bigfoot. What do you want to learn? Look up sightings on the web, or check out a book from the library. What explanations can you find?

## CREATE

**ART TIME.** Can you draw Bigfoot? Look up a picture and grab some markers and paper. Will a person see it? What will it be doing? Will it leave behind any clues? The sky is the limit!

## SHARE

**THE MORE WHO KNOW.** Share what you learned about Bigfoot. Use your own words to write a paragraph. What are the main ideas of this book? What facts from the book can you use to support those ideas? Share your paragraph with a classmate. Do they have any comments or questions?

## GROW

**DISCOVER!** The world is so big. There could be anything out there. Go on a hike with your family. What can you find? Are there animal tracks? Can you find any signs of Bigfoot?

# RESEARCH NINJA

Visit *www.ninjaresearcher.com/4835* to learn how
to take your research skills and book report writing to the next level!

## Research

**DIGITAL LITERACY TOOLS**

### SEARCH LIKE A PRO
Learn how to use search engines to find useful websites.

### FACT OR FAKE
Discover how you can tell a trusted website from an untrustworthy resource.

### TEXT DETECTIVE
Explore how to zero in on the information you need most.

### SHOW YOUR WORK
Research responsibly—learn how to cite sources.

## Write

**DOWNLOADABLE BOOK REPORT FORMS**

### GET TO THE POINT
Learn how to express your main ideas.

### PLAN OF ATTACK
Learn prewriting exercises and create an outline.

# FURTHER RESOURCES

## BOOKS

Cole, Bradley. *Bigfoot*. North Mankato, Minn.: Capstone Press, 2020.

Jones, Molly. *Bigfoot*. New York, NY: AV2 by Weigl, 2020.

Teitelbaum, Michael. *Tracking Big Foot: Is It Real or a Hoax?* New York, NY: Children's Press, 2020.

## WEBSITES

### FACTSURFER

Factsurfer.com gives you a safe, fun way to find more information.

1. Go to www.factsurfer.com.

2. Enter "Bigfoot" into the search box and click 🔍

3. Select your book cover to see a list of related websites.

# GLOSSARY

**apex predator:** a predator at the top of a food chain that is not hunted by any other animal.

**biped:** a two-footed creature.

**camouflage:** a disguise or natural coloring that allows something to hide by making it look like its surroundings.

**communicating:** sharing information with another through language, sounds, eye contact, or gestures.

**DNA:** the material in the body that carries all the information about how a living thing will look, grow, and function.

**elusive:** very hard to find or capture.

**evidence:** information and facts that help prove something is true or false.

**legend:** a story handed down from earlier times. Legends are often based on fact, but they are not entirely true.

**Neanderthals:** human-like creatures that lived from about 30,000 to 200,000 years ago.

**remote:** secluded or isolated.

**species:** one of the groups into which similar living things belong. Members of the same species are able to produce young.

**territorial:** guards or defends one's area.

# INDEX

## PHOTO CREDITS

# ABOUT THE AUTHOR

Jenna Lee Gleisner is a children's book author and editor who lives in Minnesota. In her spare time, she likes to hike, read, research fun topics like Bigfoot, and spend time with her dog, Norrie.